1st Grade Jumbo Workbook

Spelling, Reading & Math

Speedy Publishing LLC
40 E. Main St. #1156
Newark, DE 19711
www.speedypublishing.com

Spelling

E _ _ _ _ _ _ _

G _ _ _

F _ _ _

C _ _

A _ _ _ _

D _ _ _ _ _ _ _

𝓑 _ _

I _ _ _ _ _ _ _

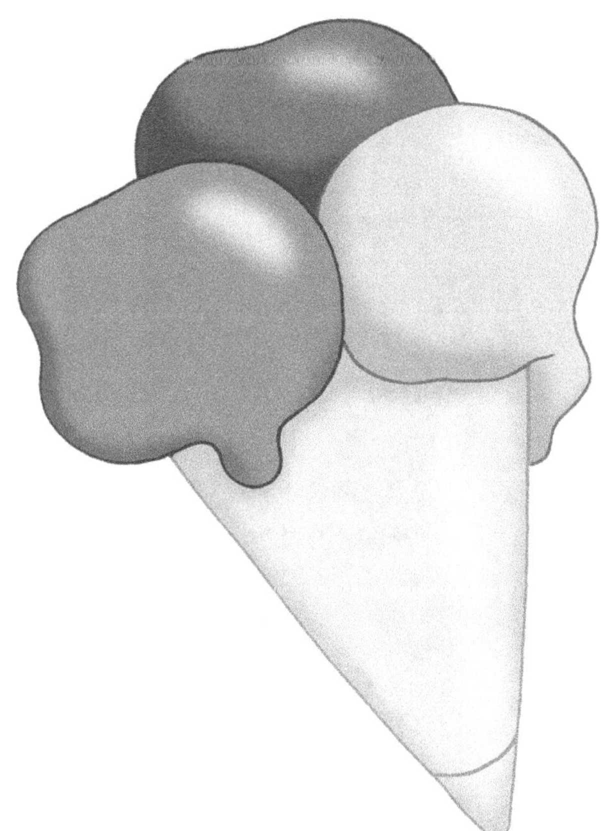

J _ _ _ _

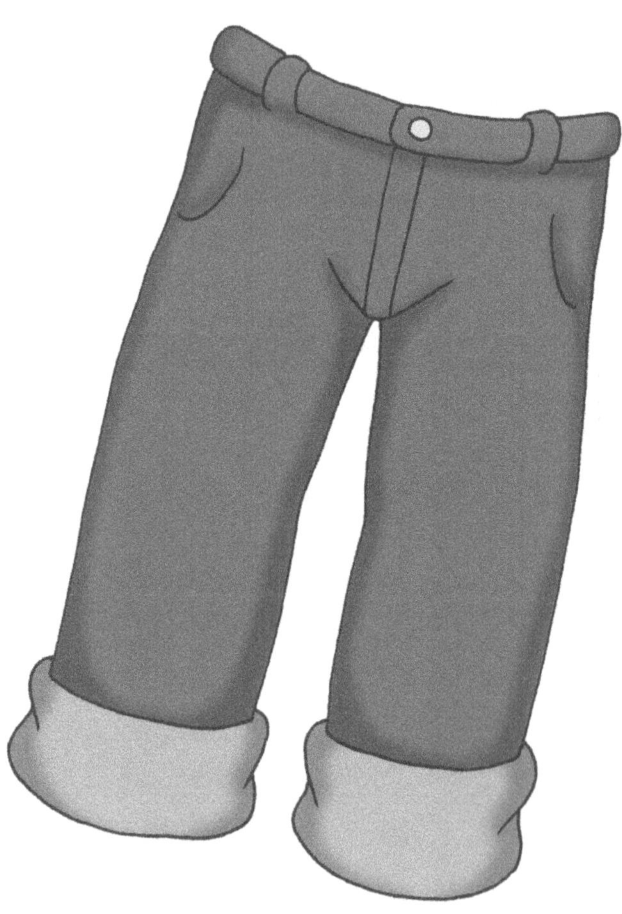

M _ _ _ _ _ _ _

K _ _

O _ _ _ _ _

L _ _ _

N _ _ _

T _ _ _ _ _

P _ _

S _ _ _ _

Q _ _ _ _

R _ _

W_ _ _

Z _ _ _ _

v_ _ _ _

u _ _ _ _ _ _ _

y_ _ _ _

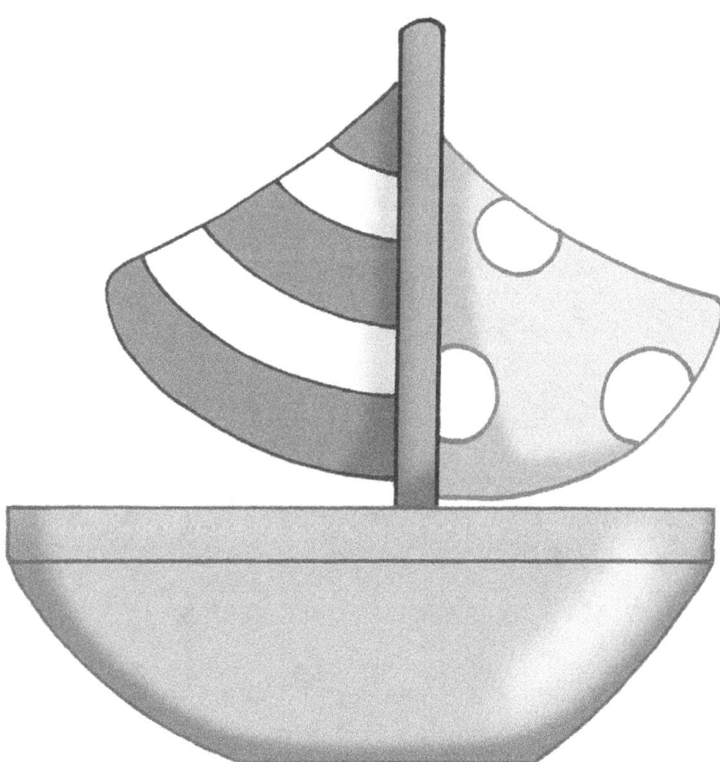

*H*_ _ _ _ _ _

Color and Identify

C_t_e_p__la_

A_l__a_or

B _ _ _

E _ _ _ _ ant

F_o_

G _ _ _

H _ _ _ e

J _ ll _ _ is _

K _ n _ a _ _ o

L _ _ n

Mo _ _ _

O_t_p_s

R___it

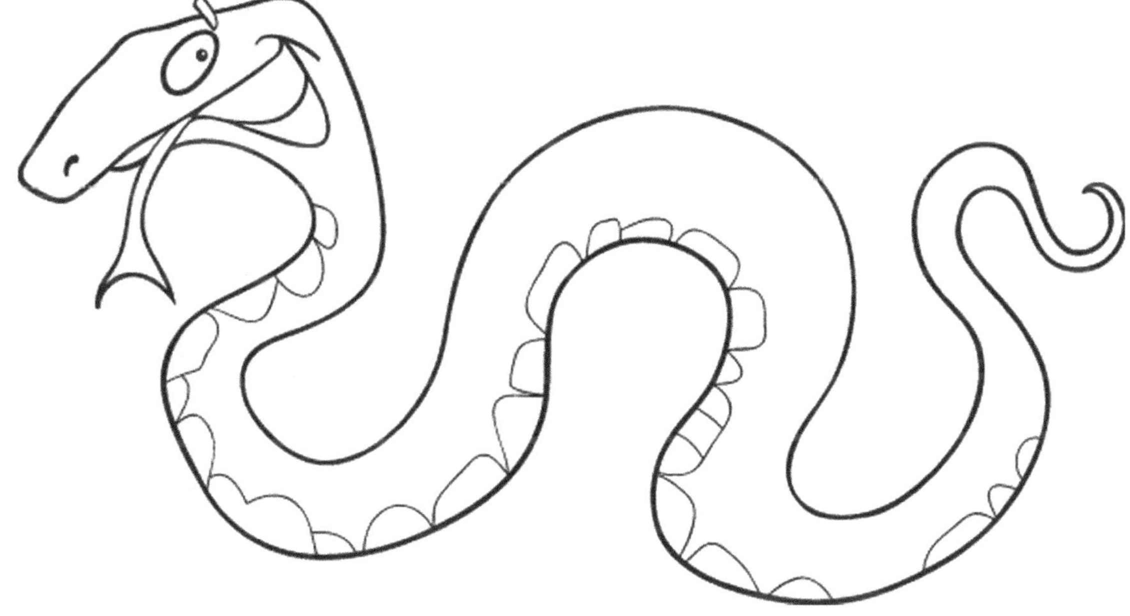

S _ _ _ e

z _ _ _ a

Reading and Tracing

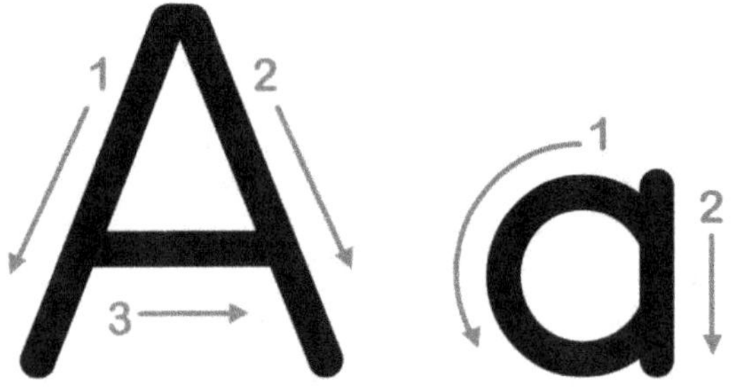

Aa Aa Aa

Ant

Arm

Acorn

Airplane

Apple

B b

Book

Bee

Ball

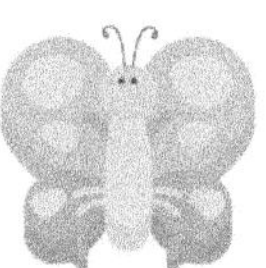

Butterfly

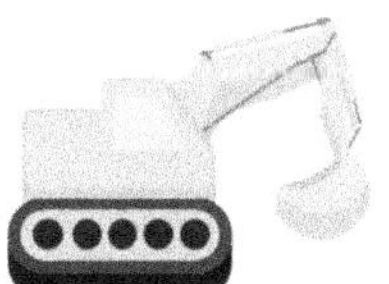

Backhoe

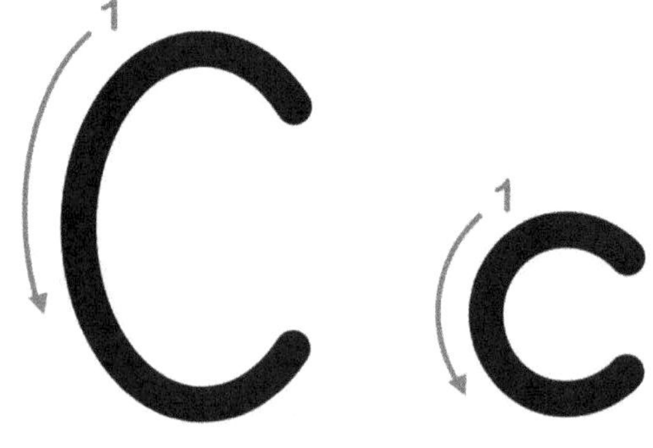

Car

Cake

Carrot

Clock

Cloud

D d

Duck

Dragonfly

Diamond

Donut

Dolphin

2
1
3
E
4
2
e
1
E e E e E e
Elephant
Egg
Earth
Eggplant
Eagle

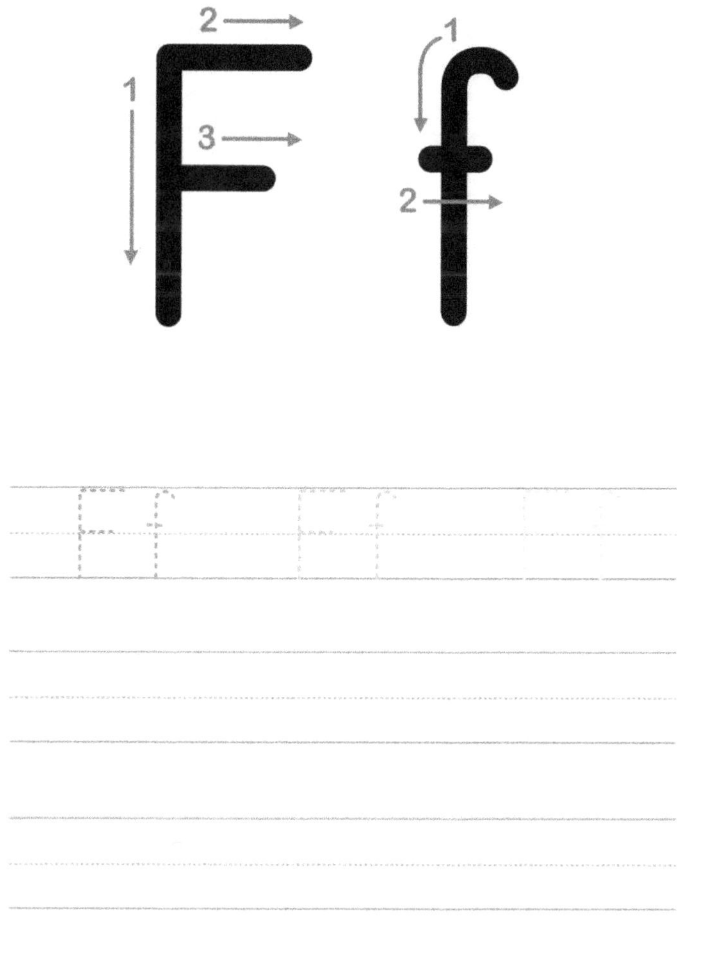

Fish

Frog

Flower

Flag

Fork

Grapes

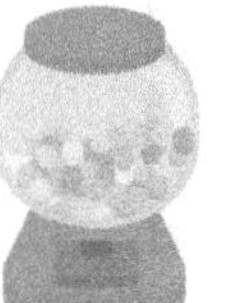

Gumball

Ghost

Giraffe

Gift

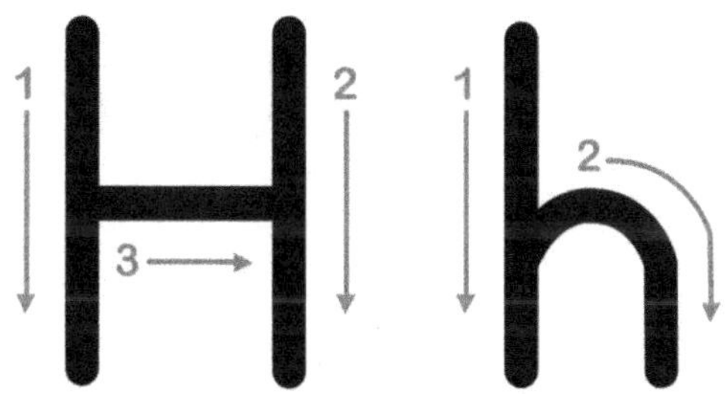
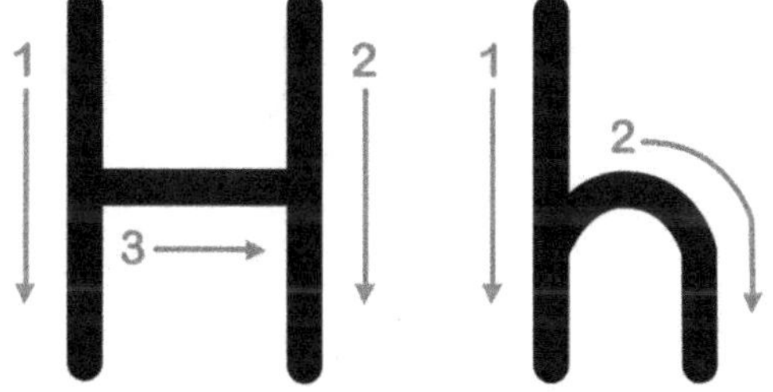

Hh Hh Hh

Hat

Hand

Heart

House

Hippopotamus

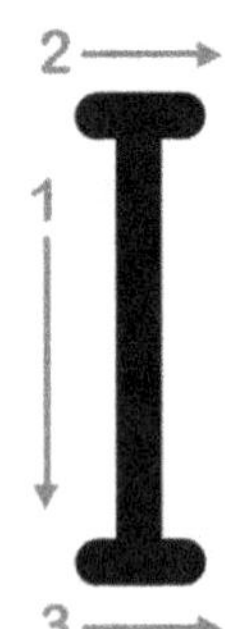

Ice Cream

Igloo

Iguana

Ice

Ink

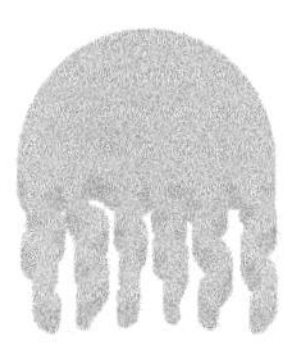

Jellyfish

Jam

Jelly

Jacket

Jigsaw

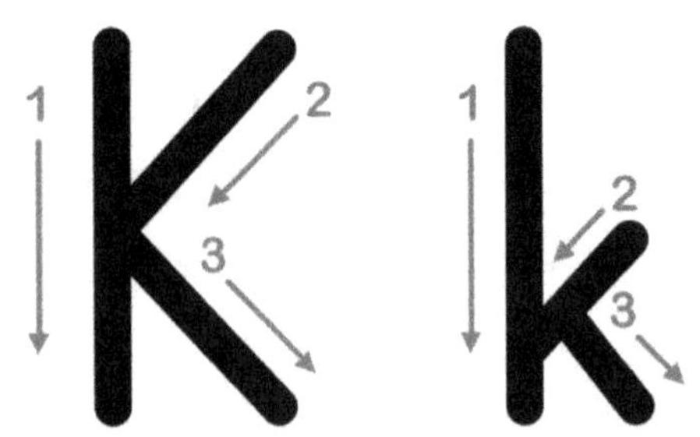

Kangaroo

Koala

Key

Knife

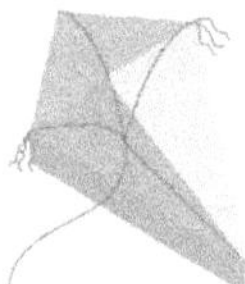

Kite

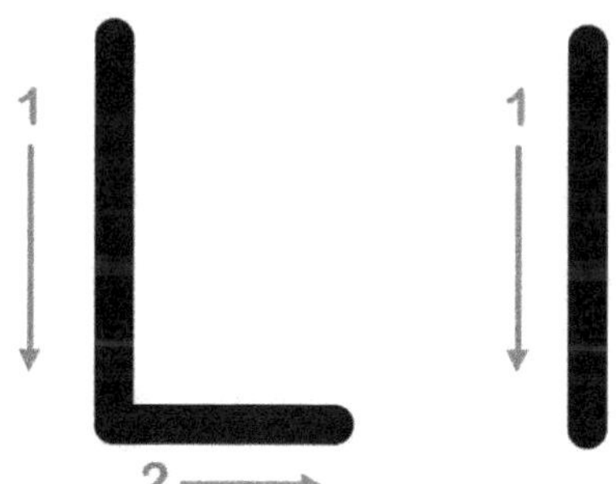

ion

etter

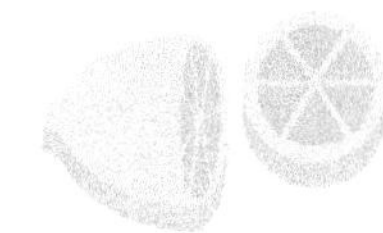

emon

eaf

adybug

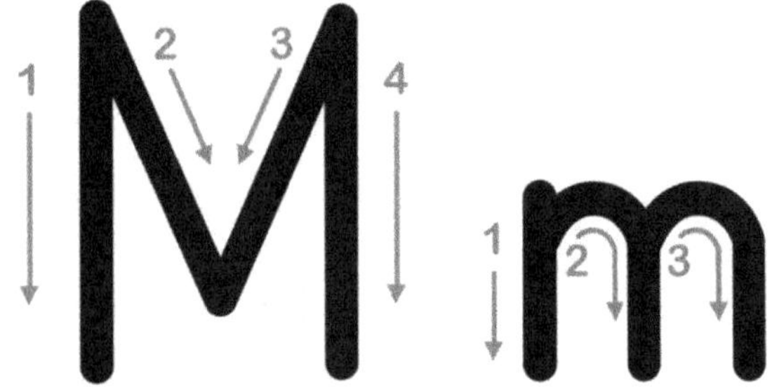

Moon

Monkey

Milk

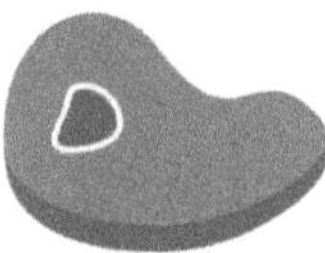

Meat

Mushroom

Nn

1 2 3

1 2

Nn Nn Nn

Necklace

Nest

Note

Nail

Notebook

O o

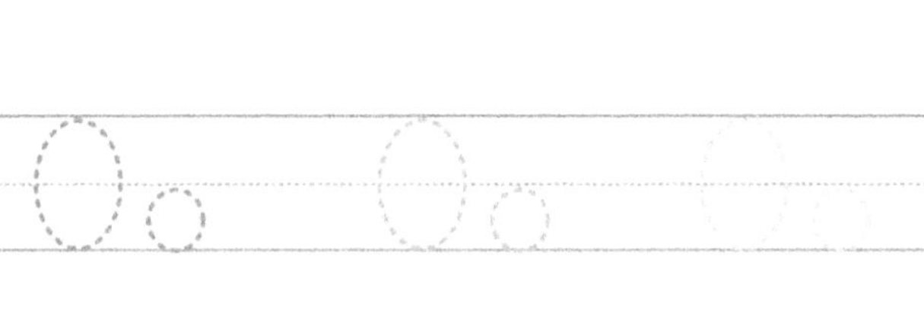

ctopus

range

strich

rchid

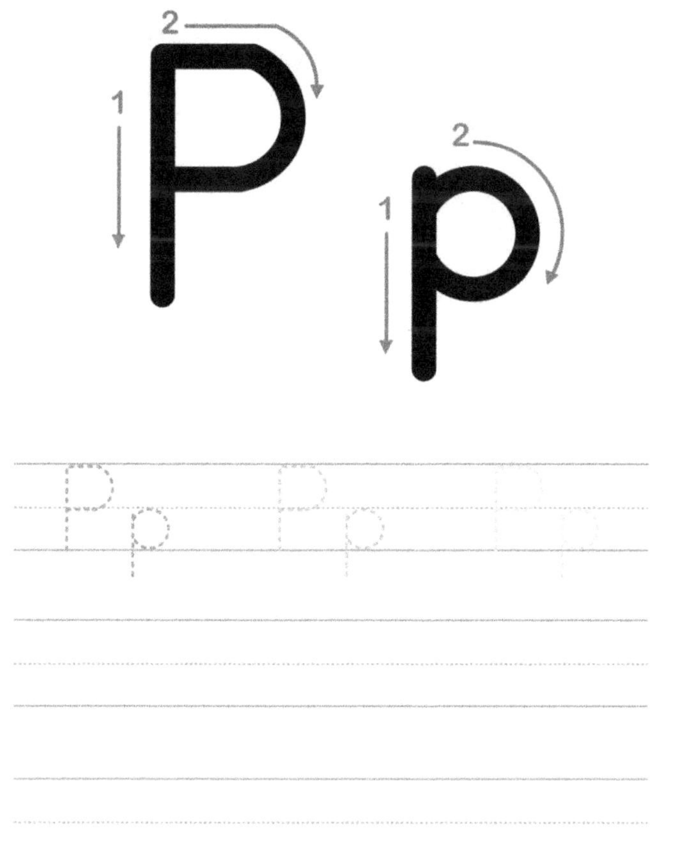

Pan

Pig

Pencil

Penguin

Peacock

Q q

Question

Queen

Quail

Quilt

Quill

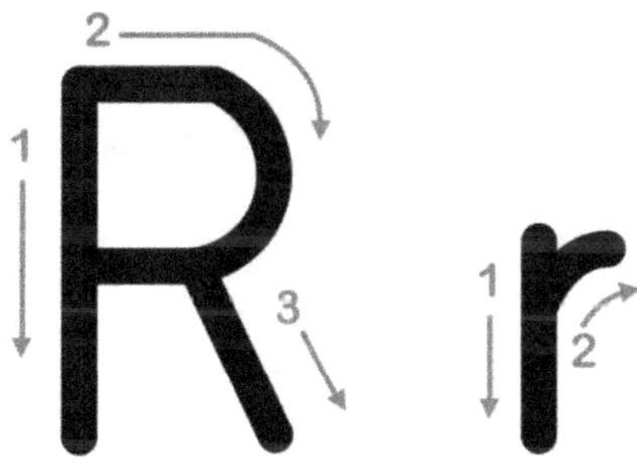

Rr Rr

Rabbit

Robot

Rainbow

Ring

Rocking horse

S s

S s S s

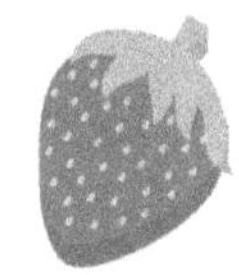

Strawberry

Shirt

Slide

Snail

Sun

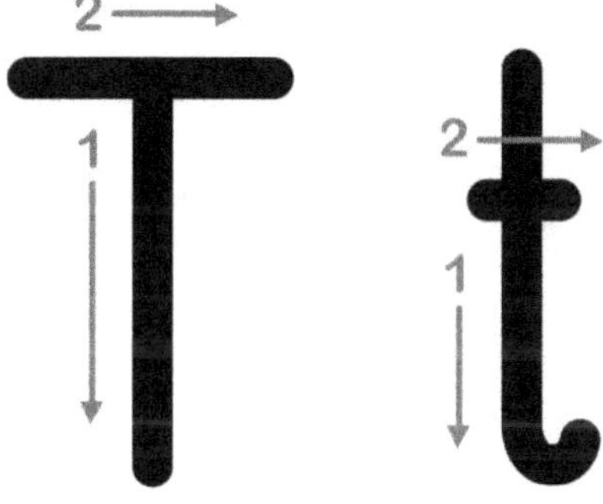

Tiger

Tablet

Turtle

Tennis

Tree

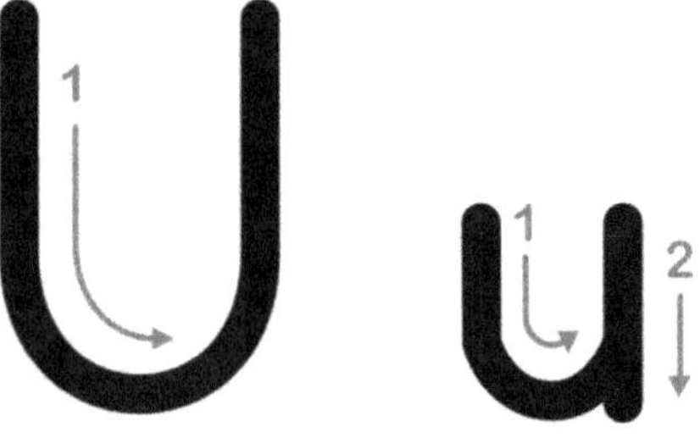

Umbrella

Unlock

Unicorn

UFO

Underwear

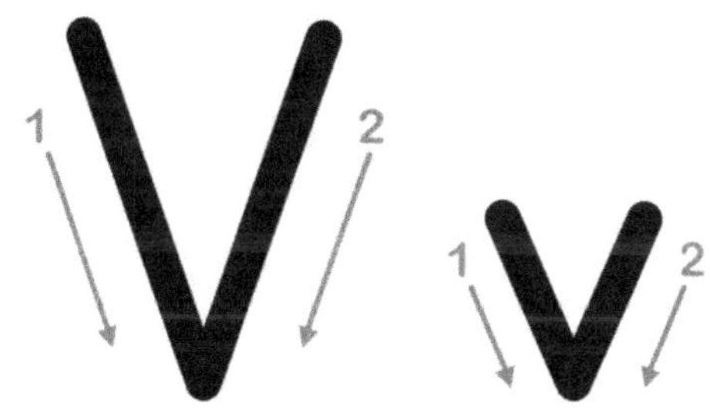

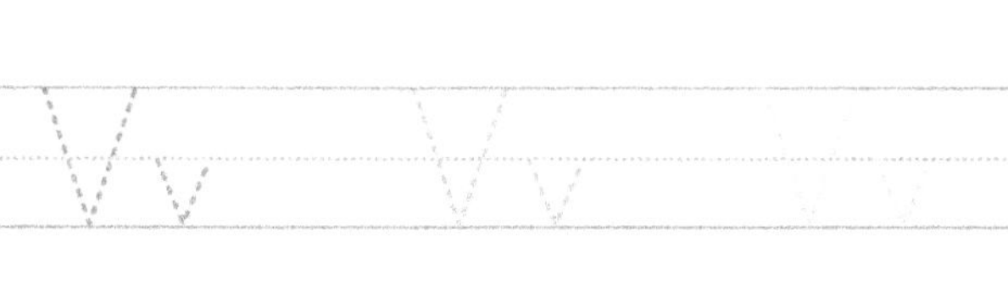

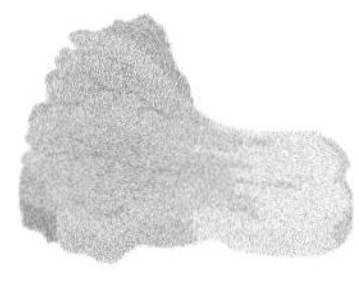

Vegetable

Van

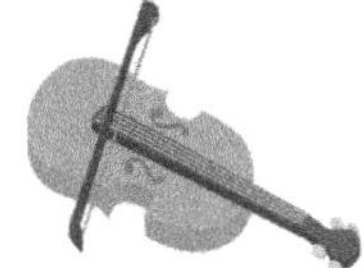

Violin

Vase

Volcano

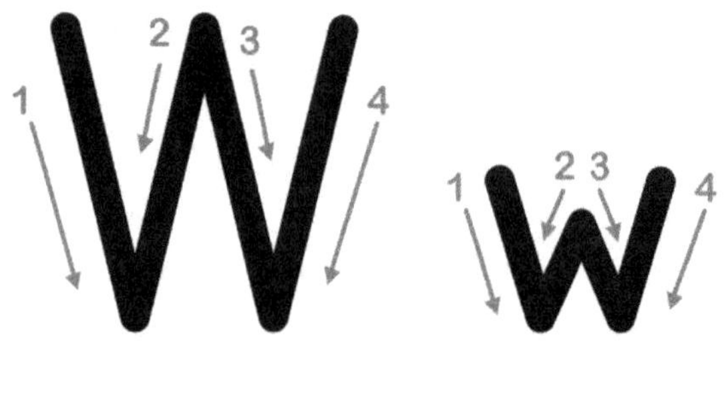

Ww Ww Ww

Whale

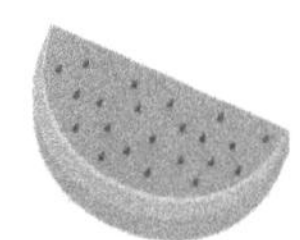

Watermelon

Wagon

Worm

Weathercock

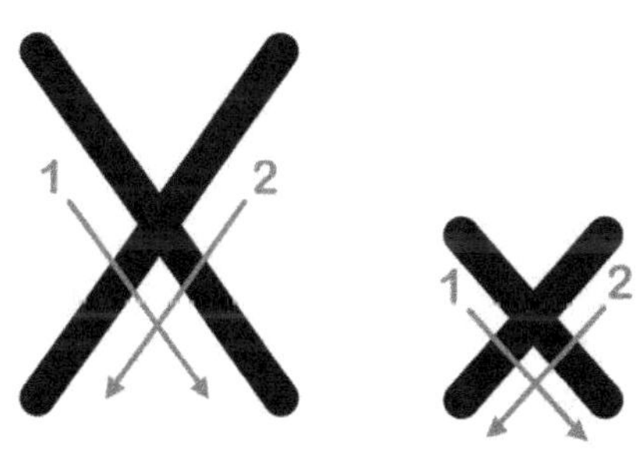

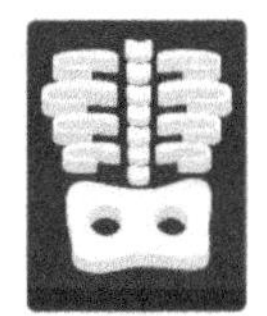

X-ray

X'mas **tree**

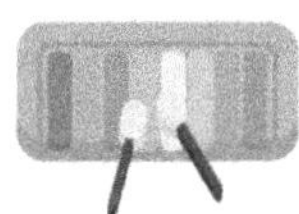

Xylophone

Xerus

Xiphias

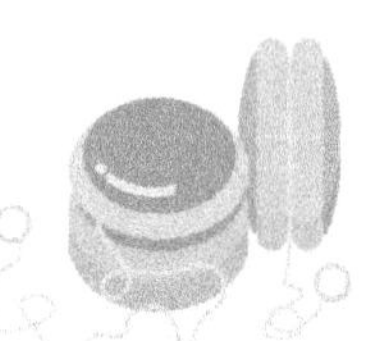

Yo-yo

Yellow

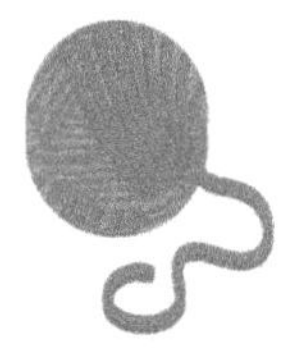

Yarn

Yacht

Yak

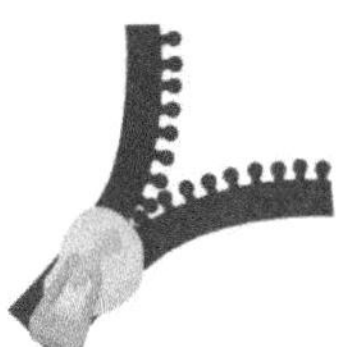

Zip

Zebra

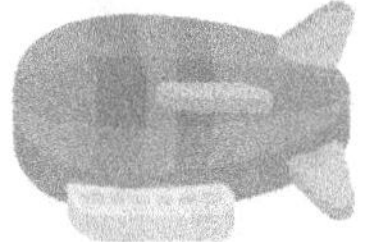

Zeppelin

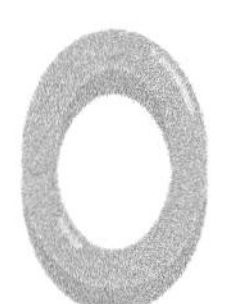

Zero

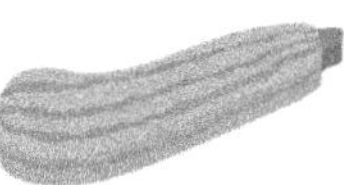

Zucchini

Math

Name: Score:

SIMPLE ADDITION

$$\begin{array}{r} 7 \\ +\ \ 4 \\ \hline \end{array} \qquad \begin{array}{r} 2 \\ +\ \ 9 \\ \hline \end{array} \qquad \begin{array}{r} 5 \\ +\ \ 8 \\ \hline \end{array}$$

$$\begin{array}{r} 1 \\ +\ \ 8 \\ \hline \end{array} \qquad \begin{array}{r} 7 \\ +\ \ 7 \\ \hline \end{array} \qquad \begin{array}{r} 6 \\ +\ \ 9 \\ \hline \end{array}$$

Name: Score:

SIMPLE ADDITION

$$\begin{array}{r} 9 \\ +\ 5 \\ \hline \end{array} \qquad \begin{array}{r} 9 \\ +\ 3 \\ \hline \end{array} \qquad \begin{array}{r} 8 \\ +\ 5 \\ \hline \end{array}$$

$$\begin{array}{r} 2 \\ +\ 8 \\ \hline \end{array} \qquad \begin{array}{r} 6 \\ +\ 0 \\ \hline \end{array} \qquad \begin{array}{r} 6 \\ +\ 7 \\ \hline \end{array}$$

Name: Score:

SIMPLE ADDITION

7 + 5	8 + 6	4 + 5
4 + 1	2 + 3	4 + 2

Name: Score:

SIMPLE ADDITION

```
   4        2        6
+  1     +  4     +  3
____     ____     ____

   5        6        5
+  8     +  2     +  1
____     ____     ____
```

Name: Score:

SIMPLE ADDITION

$$\begin{array}{r} 8 \\ +\ 4 \\ \hline \end{array} \qquad \begin{array}{r} 7 \\ +\ 3 \\ \hline \end{array} \qquad \begin{array}{r} 6 \\ +\ 2 \\ \hline \end{array}$$

$$\begin{array}{r} 2 \\ +\ 6 \\ \hline \end{array} \qquad \begin{array}{r} 3 \\ +\ 7 \\ \hline \end{array} \qquad \begin{array}{r} 4 \\ +\ 1 \\ \hline \end{array}$$

Name: Score:

SIMPLE SUBTRACTION

3	5	8
- 2	- 1	- 0
4	5	6
- 1	- 2	- 3

Name: **Score:**

SIMPLE SUBTRACTION

9	10	5
- 2	- 1	- 4
8	9	7
- 2	- 3	- 4

Name: Score:

SIMPLE SUBTRACTION

11 - 2	8 - 4	5 - 5
7 - 5	8 - 5	12 - 3

Name: Score:

SIMPLE SUBTRACTION

7 - 7	8 - 7	15 - 6
12 - 4	8 - 1	7 - 2

Name: Score:

SIMPLE SUBTRACTION

7 - 4	10 - 1	9 - 3
13 - 4	6 - 3	4 - 1

Name: **Score:**

COUNT FORWARDS

by 3S

1. 3 , 6 , 9 , 12 , ____ , ____ , ____

2. 1 , 4 , 7, 10 , ____ ,____ ,____

3. 5 , 8 , 11 , 14 , ____ ,____ ,____ ,

4. 11 , 14 , 17 , 20 , ____ ,____ ,____ ,

Name: Score:

COUNT FORWARDS

by 4S

1. 4 , 8 , 12 , 16 , ____ , ____ , ____

2. 2 , 6, 10 , 14 , ____ ,____ ,____

3. 5 , 9 , 13 , 17 , ____ ,____ ,____ ,

4. 7 , 11 , 15 , 19 , ____ ,____ ,____ ,

Name: Score:

COUNT FORWARDS

by 5S

1. 5 , 10 , 15 , 20 , ____ , ____ , ____

2. 7 , 12 , 17, 22 , ____ ,____ ,____

3. 9 , 14 , 19 , 24 , ____ ,____ ,____ ,

4. 8 , 13 , 18 , 23 , ____ ,____ ,____ ,

Name: **Score:**

COMPARING NUMBERS

Write the “**<**”, “>” or “=” symbol

1. 1 3

2. 9 6

3. 4 4

4. 10 3

5. 8 8

6. 5 6

7. 2 8

8. 6 6

Name: Score:

COMPARING NUMBERS

Write the "**<**", ">" or "=" symbol

1. 4 9

2. 2 1

3. 4 7

4. 9 10

5. 7 2

6. 8 3

7. 1 8

8. 5 2

Name:

Score:

COMPARING NUMBERS

Write the “**<**”, “>” or “=” symbol

1. 12 14

2. 2 8

3. 6 3

4. 7 7

5. 4 1

6. 5 9

7. 11 8

8. 5 6

Name: **Score:**

COMPARING NUMBERS

Write the “**<**”, “>” or “=” symbol

1. 8 3

2. 4 6

3. 8 7

4. 9 9

5. 7 1

6. 8 4

7. 9 8

8. 3 2

Name: **Score:**

COMPARING NUMBERS

Write the “**<**”, “>” or “=” symbol

1. 4 4

2. 2 6

3. 3 3

4. 9 5

5. 3 2

6. 12 3

7. 14 8

8. 10 10

Name: Score:

COMPLETE THE NUMBERS

1		3	4	5
6	7		9	
11	12		14	15
	17	18		20
21			24	25

Name: Score:

COMPLETE THE NUMBERS

6		8	9	10
11	12	13		15
16		18	19	
21		23		25
		28	29	

Name: Score:

COMPLETE THE NUMBERS

9		11		13
14	15		17	18
	20	21		23
24		26		28
29		31	32	

Name: Score:

COMPLETE THE NUMBERS

12	13		15	16
17		19	20	
22	23		25	
	28		30	31
	33	34		36

Name: Score:

COMPLETE THE NUMBERS

16		18	19	
21	22		24	
	27		29	30
	32	33		
36	37		39	40

Name: **Score:**

WORD PROBLEMS

1. Salve picked 2 apples and Tom picked 5 apples. John picked 2 apples. How many apples were picked in all?

2. For Christmas, Faye had 10 pieces of candy. She ate 2 pieces. How many pieces of candy were left?

Name: **Score:**

WORD PROBLEMS

1. Daryl's high school team played 6 basketball games this year. He attended 2 games. How many basketball games did Daryl miss?

2. A book store had 10 books in the bargain bin. If they sold 3 books, but then put 2 more books in the bin. How many books would be in the bin?

Name: **Score:**

WORD PROBLEMS

1. Tom ran for 6 minutes and Ivan ran for 4 minutes. How many minutes did the boys run in all?

2. Kyle had 2 books. If he sold 1 of them and used the money he earned to buy 2 new books, how many books would Kyle have?

Name: **Score:**

WORD PROBLEMS

1. Sheila had 7 playing cards, and 3 were torn. Keith bought 2 of his cards. How many playing cards Sheila have now?

2. A teacher had 7 worksheets to grade. If she graded 4, how many worksheets would she have to grade?

Name: **Score:**

WORD PROBLEMS

1. Gwen had 8 biscuits, she gave 4 to her sister, how many biscuits are left for her?

2. Jan had 10 balloons. 6 are green and the rest are blue. How many balloons are blue?

Name: Score:

WORD PROBLEMS

1. Sheena ate 8 cookies while Charie ate 4 cookies. How many more cookies did Sheena eat than Charie?

2. Kenji got 4 new shirts as birthday gifts. If he already 5, how many shirts does he have now?

Name: **Score:**

WORD PROBLEMS

1. Jane has 3 cats. May has 4 cats. How many cats do both of them have?

2. I built 9 snowmen in the field. If 3 melted, how many is left?

Name: **Score:**

WORD PROBLEMS

1. I have 3 pencils in the can. The can fits 10 pencils, how many more pencils can fit?

2. Grace had 10 sweets but she gave Jenna 4. How many is left?

ANSWERS

p.73 11
11
13
9
14
15

p.74 14
12
13
10
6
13

p.75 12
14
9
5
5
6

p.76 5
6
9
13
8
6

p.77 12
10
8
8
10
5

p.78 1
4
8
3
3
3

p.79 7
9
1
6
6
3

p80 9
4
0
2
3
9

p.81 0
1
9
8
7
5

p.82 3
9
6
9
3
3

Page	Answer
p.83	15,18,21
	13,16,19
	17,20,23
	23,26,29
p.84	20,24,28
	18, 22,26
	21,25,29
	23,27,31
p.85	25,30,35
	27,32,37
	29,34,39
	28,33,38
p.86	30,36,42
	33, 39,45
	29,35,41
	34,40,46
p.87	35,42,49
	29,36,43
	33,40,47
	39,46,53
p.88	>
	>
	=
	>
	=
	<
	<
	=
p.89	<
	>
	<
	<
	>
	>
	<
	>
p.90	<
	<
	>
	=
	>
	<
	>
	<
p.91	>
	<
	>
	=
	>
	>
	>
	>
p.92	=
	<
	=
	>
	>
	>
	>
	=
p.96	2+5+2=9
	10-2=8
p.97	6-2=4
	10-3+2=9
p.98	6+4=10
	2-1+2=3
p.99	7-3+2=6
	7-4=3
p.100	8-4=4
	10-6=4
p.101	8-4=4
	4+5=9
p.102	3+4=7
	9-3=6
p.103	10-3=7
	10-4=6